Microsoft PowerPoint 2016 Keyboard Shortcuts

For Windows

By

U. C-Abel Books.

Table of Contents

Acknowledgement.

U. C-Abel Books will not take all the credits for Microsoft PowerPoint 2016 keyboard shortcuts listed in this book, but shares it with Microsoft Corporation because some of the shortcut keys came from them and are "used with permission from Microsoft".

Dedication

This book is dedicated to computer users and lovers of keyboard shortcuts all over the world.

Introduction.

We enjoy using shortcut keys because they set us on a high plane that astonishes people around us when we work with them. As wonderful shortcuts users, the worst eyesore we witness in computing is to see somebody sluggishly struggling to execute a task through mouse usage when in actual sense shortcuts will help to save that person the time wasted. Most people have asked us to help them with a list of shortcut keys that can make them work as smartly as we do and that drove us into research to broaden our knowledge and truly help them as they demanded, that is the reason for the existence of this book. It is a great tool for lovers of shortcuts, and those who want to join the group.

Most times, the things we love don't come by easily. It is our love for keyboard shortcuts that made us to bear long sleepless nights like owls, just to make sure we get the best out of it, and it is the best we got that we are sharing with you in this book. You cannot be the same at computing after reading this book. The time you entrusted to our care is an expensive possession and we promise not to mess it up.

Thank you.

What to Know Before You Begin.

General Notes.

1. It is important to note that when using shortcuts to perform any command, you should make sure the target area is active, if not, you may get a wrong result. Example, if you want to highlight all texts, you must make sure the text field is active and if an object, make sure the object area is active. The active area is always known by the location where the cursor of your computer blinks.

2. Most of the keyboard shortcuts you will see in this book refer to the U.S. keyboard layout. Keys for other layouts might not correspond exactly to the keys on a U.S. keyboard.

3. The plus (+) signs that come in the middle of keyboard shortcuts simply mean the keys are meant to be combined or held down together not to be added as one of the shortcut keys. In a case where plus sign is needed; it will be duplicated (++).

4. For keyboard shortcuts in which you press one key immediately followed by another key, the keys are separated by a comma (,).

5. It is also important to note that the shortcut keys listed in this book are for Microsoft PowerPoint 2016.

Short Forms Used in This Book and Their Full Meaning.

The following are short forms of keyboard shortcuts used in this Microsoft PowerPoint 2016 Keyboard Shortcuts book and their full meaning.

1. Alt   -   Alternate Key
2. Caps Lock   -   Caps Lock Key
3. Ctrl   -   Control Key
4. Esc   -   Escape Key
5. F   -   Function Key
6. Num Lock   -   Number Lock Key
7. Shft   -   Shift Key
8. Tab   -   Tabulate Key
9. Win   -   Windows logo key
10. Prt sc   -   Print Screen

CHAPTER 1.

Gathering The Basic Knowledge Of Keyboard Shortcuts.

Without the existence of the keyboard, there wouldn't have been anything like keyboard shortcuts, so in this chapter we will learn a little about keyboard before moving to keyboard shortcuts.

1. Definition of Computer Keyboard.
This is an input device that is used to send data to the computer memory.

Sketch of a Keyboard

1.1 Types of Keyboard.

   i. Standard (Basic) Keyboard.
   ii. Enhanced (Extended) Keyboard.

i. **Standard Keyboard:** This is a keyboard designed during the 1800s for mechanical typewriters with just 10 function keys (F keys) placed at the left side of it.

ii. **Enhanced Keyboard:** This is the current 101 to 102-key keyboard that is included in almost all the personal computers (PCs) of nowadays, which has 12 function keys at the top side of it.

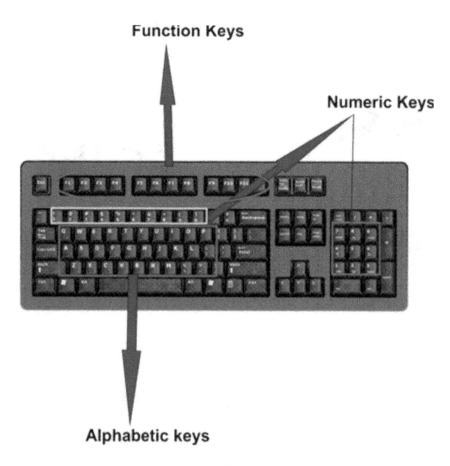

Function Keys

Numeric Keys

Alphabetic keys

1.2 Segments of the keyboard

- Numeric keys
- Alphabetic keys
- Punctuation keys
- Windows Logo key.
- Function keys
- Special keys

Numeric Keys: Numeric keys are keys with numbers from **0 - 9**.

Alphabetic Keys: These are keys that have alphabets on them, ranging from **A-Z**.

Punctuation Keys: These are keys of the keyboard used for punctuation. Examples include comma, full stop, colon, question marks, hyphen etc.

Windows Logo Key: A key on Microsoft Computer keyboard with its logo displayed on it. Search for this ⊞ on your keyboard.

Function Keys: These are keys that have **F** on them which are usually combined with other keys. They are F1 - F12, and are also in the class called Special Keys.

Special Keys: These are keys that perform special functions. They include: Tab, Ctrl, Caps lock, Insert,

Prt sc, alt gr, Shift, Home, Num lock, Esc and many others. Special keys work according to the type of computer involved. In some keyboard layout, especially laptops, the keys that turn the speaker on/off, the one that increases/decreases volume, the key that turns the computer Wifi on/off are also special keys.

Other Special Keys Worthy of Note.

Enter Key: This is located at the right-hand corner of the keyboard. It is used to send messages to the computer to execute commands, in most cases it is used to mean "Ok" or "Go".

Escape Key (ESC): This is the first key on the upper left of the keyboard. It is used to cancel routines, close menus and select options such as **Save** according to circumstance.

Control Key (CTRL): It is located on the bottom row of the left and right hand side of the keyboard. They also work with the function keys to execute commands using Keyboard shortcuts (key combinations).

Alternate Key (ALT): It is located on the bottom row, very close to the CTRL key on both side of the keyboard. It enables many editing functions to be accomplished by using some keystroke combinations on the keyboard.

Shift Key: This adds to the functions of the function keys. In addition, it enables the use of alternative function of a particular button (key), especially, those with more than one function on a key. E.g. use of capital letters, symbols and numbers.

1.3. Selecting/Highlighting With the Keyboard.

This is a highlighting method or style where data is selected using the keyboard instead of a computer mouse.

To do this:

- Move your cursor to the text you want to highlight, make sure that area is active,
- Hold down the shift key with one finger
- Then use another finger to move the arrow key that points to the direction you want to highlight.

1.4 The Operating Modes Of The Keyboard.

Just like the mouse the keyboard has two operating modes. The two modes are Text Entering and Command Mode.

a. **Text Entering Mode:** this mode gives the operator/user the opportunity to type text.

b. **Command Mode:** this is used to command the operating system/software/application to execute commands in certain ways.

2. Ways To Improve In Your Typing Skill.

1. Put Your Eyes Off The Keyboard.

This is the aspect of keyboard usage that many don't find funny because they always ask. "How can I put my eyes off the keyboard when I am running away from the occurrence of errors on my file?" My aim is to be fast, is this not going to slow me down?

Of course, there will be errors and at the same time your speed will slow down but the motive behind the introduction of this method is to make you faster than you are. Looking at your keyboard while you type can make you get a sore neck, it is better you learn to touch type because the more you type with your eyes fixed on the screen instead of the keyboard, the faster you become.

An alternative to keeping your eyes off your keyboard is to use the *"Das Keyboard Ultimate"*.

2. Errors Challenge You

It is better to fail than not to try at all. Not trying at all is an attribute of the weak and lazybones. When you make mistakes, try again because errors are opportunities for improvement.

3. Good Posture (Position Yourself Well).
Do not adopt an awkward position while typing. You should get everything on your desk organized or arranged before sitting to type. Your posture while typing contributes to your speed and productivity.

4. Practice
Here is the conclusion of everything said above. You have to practice your shortcuts constantly. The practice alone is a way of improvement. "Practice brings improvement". Practice always.

2.1 Software That Will Help You Improve In Your Typing Skill.

There are several Software programs for typing that both kids and adults can use for their typing skill. Here is a list of software that can help you improve in your typing: Mavis Beacon, Typing Instructor, Mucky Typing Adventure, Rapid Tying Tutor, Letter Chase Tying Tutor, Alice Touch Typing Tutor and many more. Personally, I recommend Mavis Beacon.

To learn typing with MAVIS BEACON, install Mavis Beacon software to your computer, start with keyboard lesson, then move to games. Games like **Penguin Crossing, Creature Lab** or **Space Junk** will help you become a professional in typing. Typing and keyboard shortcuts work hand-in-hand.

Sketch of a computer mouse

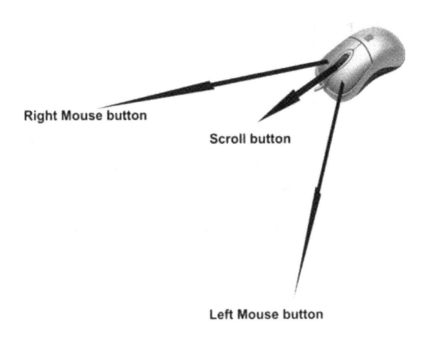

Right Mouse button

Scroll button

Left Mouse button

3. Mouse:

This is an oval-shaped portable input device with three buttons for scrolling, left clicking, and right clicking that enables work to be done effectively on a computer. The plural form of mouse is mice.

3.1 Types of Computer Mouse

- Mechanical Mouse
- Optical Mechanical Mouse (Optomechanical)
- Laser Mouse
- Optical Mouse

- BlueTrack Mouse

3.2 Forms of Clicking:

Left Clicking: This is the process of clicking the left side button of the mouse. It can be called *clicking* without the addition of *left*.

Right Clicking: It is the process of clicking the right side button of the mouse.

Double Clicking: It is the process of clicking the left side button two times (twice) and immediately.

Double clicking is used to select a word while thrice clicking is used to select a sentence or paragraph.

Scroll Button: It is the little key attached to the mouse that looks like a tiny wheel. It takes you up and down a page when moved.

3.3 Mouse Pad: This is a small soft mat that is placed under the mouse to make it have a free movement.

3.4 Laptop Mouse Touchpad

This unlike the mouse we explained above is not external, rather it is inbuilt (comes with a laptop computer). With the presence of a laptop mouse touchpad, an external mouse is not needed to use a laptop, except in a case where it is malfunctioning or the operator prefers to use external one for some reasons.

The laptop mouse touchpad is usually positioned at the end of the keyboard section of a laptop computer. It is rectangular in shape with two buttons positioned below it. The two buttons/keys are used for left and right clicking just like the external mouse. Some laptops come with four mouse keys. Two placed above the mouse for left and right clicking and two other keys placed below it for the same function.

4. Definition Of Keyboard Shortcuts.

Keyboard shortcuts are defined as a series of keys, sometimes with combination that execute tasks that typically involve the use of mouse or other input devices.

5. Why You Should Use Shortcuts.

1.   One may not be able to use a computer mouse easily because of disability or pain.

2.   One may not be able to see the mouse pointer as a result of vision impairment, in such case what will the person do? The answer is SHORTCUT.

3. Research has made it known that Extensive mouse usage is related to Repetitive Syndrome Injury (RSI) greatly than the use of keyboard.

4. Keyboard shortcuts speed up computer users, making learning them a worthwhile effort.

5. When performing a job that requires precision, it is wise that you use the keyboard instead of mouse, for instance, if you are dealing with Text Editing, it is better you handle it using keyboard shortcuts than spending more time with mouse alone.

6. Studies calculate that using keyboard shortcuts allows working 10 times faster than working with the mouse. The time you spend looking for the mouse and then getting the cursor to the position you want is lost! Reducing your work duration by 10 times brings you greater results.

5.1 Ways To Become A Lover Of Shortcuts.

1. Always have the urge to learn new shortcut keys associated with the programs you use.
2. Be happy whenever you learn a new shortcut.
3. Try as much as you can to apply the new shortcuts you learnt.
4. Always bear it in mind that learning new shortcuts is worth it.

5. Always remember that the use of keyboard shortcuts keeps people healthy while performing computing activities.

5.2 How To Learn New Shortcut Keys

1. Do a research for them: quick reference (a cheat sheet comprehensively compiled) can go a long way to help you improve.
2. Buy applications that show you keyboard shortcuts every time you execute an action with the mouse.
3. Disconnect your mouse if you must learn this fast.
4. Read user manuals and help topics (Whether offline or online).

5.3 Your Reward For Knowing Shortcut Keys.

1. You will get faster unimaginably.
2. Your level of efficiency will increase.
3. You will find it easy to use.
4. Opportunities are high that you will become an expert in what you do.
5. You won't have to go for **Office button**, click **New,** click **Blank and Recent** and click **Create** just to insert a fresh/blank page. **Ctrl +N** takes care of that in a second.

A Funny Note: Keyboard Shortcuts and Mousing are in a marital union with Keyboard Shortcuts being the head and it will be unfair for anybody to put asunder between them.

5.4 Why We Emphasize On The Use of Shortcuts.

You may never ditch your mouse completely unless you are ready to make your brain a box of keyboard shortcuts which will really be frustrating. Just imagine yourself learning all the shortcuts for the programs you use and its various versions. You shouldn't learn keyboard shortcuts that way.

Why we are emphasizing on the use of shortcuts is because mouse usage is becoming unusually common and unhealthy, too. So we just want to make sure both are combined so you can get fast, productive and healthy in your computing activities. All you need to know is just the most important ones associated with the programs you use.

CHAPTER 2.

15 (Fifteen) Special Keyboard Shortcuts.

The fifteen special keyboard shortcuts are fifteen (15) shortcut keys every computer user should know.

The following table contains the list of keyboard shortcuts every computer user should know.

1. **Ctrl + A:** Control plus A, highlights or selects everything you have in the environment where you are working.

    *If you are like **"Wow, the content of this document is large and there is no time to select all of it, besides, it's going to mount pressure on my computer?"** Using the mouse for this is an outdated method of handling a task like selecting all, Ctrl+A will take care of that within seconds.*

2. **Ctrl + C:** Control plus C copies any highlighted or selected element within the work environment.

    Saves the time and stress which would have been used to right click and click again just to copy. Use ctrl+c.

3. **Ctrl + N:** Control plus N opens a new window. *Instead of clicking* **File, New, blank/ template** *and another* **click**, *just press* ***Ctrl + N*** *and a fresh window will appear instantly.*

4. **Ctrl + O:** Control plus O opens a new program. *Use ctrl +O when you want to locate or open a file or program.*

5. **Ctrl + P:** Control plus P prints the active document. *Always use this to locate the printer dialog box and print.*

6. **Ctrl + S:** Control plus S saves a new document or file and changes made by the user. *Going for the mouse? Please stop! Don't use the mouse. Just press Ctrl+S and everything will be saved.*

7. **Ctrl +V:** Control plus V pastes copied elements into the active area of the program in use. *Using ctrl+V in a case like this Saves the time and stress of right clicking and clicking again just to paste.*

8. **Ctrl + W:** Control plus W is used to close the page you are working on when you want to leave the work environment.

> ***"There is a way Peace does this without using the mouse. Oh my God, why didn't I learn it then?"*** Don't worry, I have the answer, Peace presses Ctrl+W to close active windows.

9. **Ctrl + X:** Control plus X cuts elements (making the elements to disappear from their original place). The difference between cutting and deleting elements is that in Cutting, what was cut doesn't get lost permanently but prepares itself so that it can be pasted in another location selected by the user.

> *Use ctrl+x when you think **"this shouldn't be here and I can't stand the stress of retyping or redesigning it in the rightful place it belongs"**.*

10. **Ctrl + Y:** Control plus Y redoes an undone action.

> *Ctrl+Z brought back what you didn't need? Press Ctrl+ Y to remove it again.*

11. **Ctrl + Z:** Control plus Z undoes actions.

Can't find what you typed now or a picture you inserted, it suddenly disappeared or you mistakenly removed it? Press Ctrl+Z to bring it back.

12. **Alt + F4:** Alternative plus F4 closes active windows or items.

   *You don't need to move the mouse in order to close an active window, just press **Alt + F4** if you are done or don't want somebody who is coming to see what you are doing.*

13. **Ctrl + F6:** Control plus F6 Navigates between open windows, making it possible for a user to see what is happening in windows that are active.
   Are you working in Microsoft Word and want to find out if the other active window where your browser is loading a page is still progressing? Use Ctrl + F6.

14. **F1:** This displays the help window.

   *Is your computer malfunctioning? Use **F1** to find help when you don't know what next to do.*

15. **F12:** This enables user to make changes to an already saved document.

F12 is the shortcut to use when you want to change the format in which you saved your existing document, password it, change its name, change the file location or destination, or make other changes to it. It will save your time.

CHAPTER 3.

Keyboard Shortcuts In PowerPoint 2016.

Definition of Program: Microsoft PowerPoint is a Microsoft Corporation program designed in 1990 used for graphic presentation.

The following list contains keyboard shortcuts that will boost your productivity in Microsoft PowerPoint.

Use Keyboard Shortcuts To Create Your Presentation.

Frequently Used Shortcuts

The following table itemizes the most frequently used shortcuts in PowerPoint.

TASK	SHORTCUT
Make selected text bold.	Ctrl+B
Change the font size for selected text.	Alt+H, F, and then S
Change the zoom for the slide.	Alt+W, Q
Cut selected text, object, or slide.	Ctrl+X
Copy selected text, object, or slide.	Ctrl+C
Paste cut or copied text, object,	Ctrl+V

or slide.	
Undo the last action.	Ctrl+Z
Save the presentation.	Ctrl+S
Insert a picture.	Alt+N, P
Insert a shape.	Alt+H, S, and then H
Select a theme.	Alt+G, H
Select a slide layout.	Alt+H, L
Go to the next slide.	Page Down
Go to the previous slide.	Page Up
Go to the Home tab.	Alt+H
Move to the Insert tab.	Alt+N
Start the slide show.	Alt+S,B
End the slide show.	Esc
Close PowerPoint.	Alt+F, X

Navigate The Ribbon With Only The Keyboard

The ribbon is the strip at the top of PowerPoint, organized by tabs. Each tab displays a different ribbon, which is made up of groups, and each group includes one or more commands.

You can navigate the ribbon with just the keyboard. Access keys are special shortcuts that let you quickly use a command on the ribbon by pressing a few keys, regardless of where you are in PowerPoint. Every command in PowerPoint can be accessed by using an access key.

There are two ways to navigate the tabs in the ribbon:

- To get to the ribbon, press Alt, and then, to move between tabs, use the Right Arrow and Left Arrow keys.
- To go directly to a tab on the ribbon, press one of the following access keys:

TASK	SHORTCUT
Open the File page.	Alt+F
Open the Home tab.	Alt+H
Open the Insert tab.	Alt+N
Open the Design tab.	Alt+G
Open the Transitions tab.	Alt+T
Open the Animations tab.	Alt+A
Open the Slide Show tab.	Alt+S
Open the Review tab.	Alt+R
Open the View tab.	Alt+W
Open the Tell me box.	Alt+Q, and then enter the search term

Note: Add-ins and other programs may add new tabs to the ribbon and may provide access keys for those tabs.

Work in ribbon tabs with the keyboard

- To move to the list of ribbon tabs, press Alt; to go directly to a tab, press a keyboard shortcut.

- To move between commands, press the Tab key or Shift+Tab. You move forward or backward through the commands in order. You can also press the arrow keys.
- Controls are activated in different ways, depending upon the type of control:
  - If the selected command is a button, to activate it, press Spacebar or Enter.
  - If the selected command is a split button (that is, a button that opens a menu of additional options), to activate it, press Alt+Down Arrow. Tab through the options. To select the current option, press Spacebar or Enter.
  - If the selected command is a list (such as the Font list), to open the list, press the Down Arrow key. Then, to move between items, press the arrow keys. When the item you want is selected, press Enter.
  - If the selected command is a gallery, to select the command, press the Spacebar or Enter. Then, tab through the items.

Tip: In galleries with more than one row of items, the Tab key moves from the beginning to the end of the current row and, when it reaches the end of the row, it moves to the beginning of the next one. Pressing the Right Arrow key at the end of the current row moves back to the beginning of the current row.

Change Focus By Using The Keyboard

The following table lists some ways to move the focus using the keyboard.

TASK	SHORTCUT
Select the active tab of the ribbon and activate the access keys.	Alt or F10. To move to a different tab, use access keys or the arrow keys.
Move the focus to commands on the ribbon.	Tab key or Shift+Tab
Move down, up, left, or right, respectively, among the items on the ribbon.	Down Arrow, Up Arrow, Left Arrow, or Right Arrow key
Expand or collapse the ribbon.	Ctrl+F1
Display the context menu for the selected item.	Shift+F10
Move the focus to a different pane.	F6
Move to the next or previous command on the ribbon.	Tab key or Shift+Tab
Activate the selected command or control on the ribbon.	Spacebar or Enter
Open the selected menu or gallery on the ribbon.	Spacebar or Enter
Open the selected list on the ribbon, such as the Font list.	Down Arrow key
Move between items in an opened menu or gallery.	Tab key
Finish modifying a value in a control on the ribbon,	Enter

and move the focus back to the document.	

Use access keys when you can see the Key Tips

In PowerPoint 2013 and later, you can use Key Tips to get to things on the ribbon. You can display Key Tips, which are the letters used to access commands, and then use them to navigate in the ribbon.

1. Press Alt. The Key Tips appear in small squares by each ribbon command.
2. To select a command, press the letter shown in the square Key Tip that appears by it. For example, press F to open the **File** Tab; H to open the **Home** Tab; N to open the **Insert** Tab, and so on.

Depending on which letter you press, you may be shown additional Key Tips. For example, if you press Alt+F, Backstage view opens on the **Info** page, which has a different set of Key Tips.

Move Between Panes

TASK	SHORTCUT
Move clockwise among panes in Normal view.	F6
Move counterclockwise among panes in Normal view.	Shift+F6
Switch between the Thumbnail	Ctrl+Shift+Tab

pane and the Outline View pane.	

Work In An Outline

TASK	SHORTCUT
Promote a paragraph.	Alt+Shift+Left Arrow
Demote a paragraph.	Alt+Shift+Right Arrow
Move selected paragraphs up.	Alt+Shift+Up Arrow
Move selected paragraphs down.	Alt+Shift+Down Arrow
Show heading level 1	Alt+Shift+1
Expand text below a heading.	Alt+Shift+Plus Sign (+)
Collapse text below a heading.	Alt+Shift+Minus Sign (-)

Work With Shapes, Pictures, Boxes, Objects, And WordArt.

Insert a shape

1. To select **Shapes**, press Alt+N, S, and then H.
2. Use the arrow keys to move through the categories of shapes, and select the shape you want.
3. Press Ctrl+Enter to insert the shape.

Insert a text box

1. Press Alt+N, X.
2. Press Ctrl+Enter to insert the text box.

Insert an object

1. To select **Object**, press Alt+N, and J .
2. To move the focus to the **Object type** list, press Tab.
3. Press Ctrl+Enter to insert the object.

Insert WordArt

1. To select **WordArt**, press Alt+N, W .
2. Use the arrow keys to select the WordArt style you want, and press Enter.
3. Type your text.

Select a shape

Note: If your cursor is within text, press Esc before using this shortcut.

- To select a single shape, press the Tab key to cycle forward (or Shift+Tab to cycle backward) through the objects until sizing handles appear on the object you want.

Group or ungroup shapes, pictures, and WordArt objects

- To group shapes, pictures, or WordArt objects, select the items that you want to group, and press Ctrl+G.
- To ungroup a group, select the group, and press Ctrl+Shift+G.

Copy the attributes of a shape

1. Select the shape with the attributes you want to copy.

   Note: If you select a shape with text, you copy the look and style of the text in addition to the attributes of the shape.

2. To copy the object attributes, press Ctrl+Shift+C.
3. To select the object you want to copy the attributes to, press the Tab key or Shift+Tab .
4. To paste the attributes of the shape to the selected object, press Ctrl+Shift+V.

Select And Edit Text And Objects

Select text and objects

TASK	SHORTCUT
Select one character to the right.	Shift+Right Arrow
Select one character to the left.	Shift+Left Arrow
Select to the end of a word.	Ctrl+Shift+Right Arrow
Select to the beginning of a word.	Ctrl+Shift+Left Arrow
Select one line up (with the cursor at the beginning of a line).	Shift+Up Arrow
Select one line down (with the cursor at the beginning of a line).	Shift+Down Arrow

Select an object (when the text inside the object is selected).	ESC
Select another object (when one object is selected).	Tab or Shift+Tab until the object you want is selected
Send object back one position.	Ctrl+Shift+[
Send object forward one position.	Ctrl+Shift+]
Select text within an object (with an object selected).	Enter
Select all objects.	Ctrl+A (on the **Slides** tab)
Play or pause media.	Ctrl+SPACE
Select all slides.	Ctrl+A (in **Slide Sorter** view)
Select all text.	Ctrl+A (on the **Outline** tab)

Delete and copy text and objects

TASK	SHORTCUT
Delete one character to the left.	Backspace
Delete one word to the left.	Ctrl+Backspace
Delete one character to the right.	Delete
Delete one word to the right. **Note:** The cursor must be between words to do this.	Ctrl+Delete
Cut selected object or text.	Ctrl+X
Copy selected object or text.	Ctrl+C

Paste cut or copied object or text.	Ctrl+V
Undo the last action.	Ctrl+Z
Redo the last action.	Ctrl+Y
Copy formatting only.	Ctrl+Shift+C
Paste formatting only.	Ctrl+Shift+V
Copy animation painter	Alt+Shift+C
Paste animation painter	Alt+Shift+V
Open **Paste Special** dialog box.	Ctrl+Alt+V

Move around in text

TASK	SHORTCUT
Move one character to the left.	Left Arrow
Move one character to the right.	Right Arrow
Move one line up.	Up Arrow
Move one line down.	Down Arrow
Move one word to the left.	Ctrl+Left Arrow
Move one word to the right.	Ctrl+Right Arrow
Move to the end of a line.	End
Move to the beginning of a line.	Home
Move up one paragraph.	Ctrl+Up Arrow
Move down one paragraph.	Ctrl+Down Arrow
Move to the end of a text box.	Ctrl+End
Move to the beginning of a text box.	Ctrl+Home
Move to the next title or body text placeholder. If it is the last placeholder on a slide, this action inserts a new slide with the same	Ctrl+Enter

slide layout as the original slide.	
Move to repeat the last **Find** action.	Shift+F4

Move around in and work in tables

TASK	SHORTCUT
Move to the next cell.	Tab
Move to the preceding cell.	Shift+Tab
Move to the next row.	Down Arrow
Move to the preceding row.	Up Arrow
Insert a tab in a cell.	Ctrl+Tab
Start a new paragraph.	Enter
Add a new row at the bottom of the table.	Tab in the bottom right table cell.

Edit a linked or embedded object

1. To select the object you want, press Tab or Shift+Tab.
2. To open the shortcut menu, press Shift+F10.
3. To select **Worksheet Object**, press the Down Arrow key until it's selected.
4. To select **Edit**, press the Right Arrow key and then press Enter.

Note: The name of the command in the shortcut menu depends on the type of embedded or linked object. For example, an embedded Microsoft Office Excel worksheet has the command **Worksheet Object**, whereas an embedded Microsoft Office Visio Drawing has the command **Visio Object**.

Format Text

Note: Select the text you want to change before using these keyboard shortcuts.

Change or resize a font

TASK	SHORTCUT
Open the **Font** dialog box to change the font.	Ctrl+Shift+F
Increase the font size.	Ctrl+Shift+Right Angle bracket (>)
Decrease the font size.	Ctrl+Shift+Left Angle bracket (<)

Apply character formatting

TASK	SHORTCUT
Open the **Font** dialog box to change the formatting of characters.	Ctrl+T
Change between sentence case, lowercase, or uppercase.	Shift+F3
Apply bold formatting.	Ctrl+B
Apply an underline.	Ctrl+U
Apply italic formatting.	Ctrl+I
Apply subscript formatting (automatic spacing).	Ctrl+Equal sign (=)
Apply superscript formatting (automatic spacing).	Ctrl+Shift+Plus sign (+)

Remove manual character formatting, such as subscript and superscript.	Ctrl+Spacebar
Insert a hyperlink.	Ctrl+K

Copy text formatting

TASK	SHORTCUT
Copy formats.	Ctrl+Shift+C
Paste formats.	Ctrl+Shift+V

Align paragraphs

TASK	SHORTCUT
Center a paragraph.	Ctrl+E
Justify a paragraph.	Ctrl+J
Left align a paragraph.	Ctrl+L
Right align a paragraph.	Ctrl+R

Custom Keyboard Shortcuts

To assign custom keyboard shortcuts to menu items, recorded macros, and Visual Basic for Applications (VBA) code in PowerPoint, you must use a third-party add-in, such as Shortcut Manager for PowerPoint, which is available from OfficeOne Add-Ins for PowerPoint.

Use Keyboard Shortcuts To Deliver Your Presentation.

This topic itemizes keyboard shortcuts for delivering your presentation in PowerPoint 2016.

- The shortcuts in this topic refer to the US keyboard layout. Keys for other layouts might not correspond exactly to the keys on a US keyboard.
- If a shortcut requires pressing two or more keys at the same time, this topic separates the keys with a plus sign (+). If you have to press one key immediately after another, the keys are separated by a comma (,).

Note: This topic assumes that JAWS users have turned off the Virtual Ribbon Menu feature.

Control Your Slide Show During The Presentation.

The following keyboard shortcuts apply while you're delivering your presentation in Slide Show (full-screen) mode. To enter **Slide Show** mode, press Alt+S, B.

TASK	SHORTCUT
Perform the next animation or advance to the next slide.	N, Enter, Page Down, Right Arrow, Down Arrow, or Spacebar
Perform the previous animation or return to the previous slide.	P, Page Up, Left Arrow, Up Arrow, or Backspace
Go to slide number.	number+Enter
Display a blank black slide,	B or Period

or return to the presentation from a blank black slide.	
Display a blank white slide, or return to the presentation from a blank white slide.	W or Comma
Stop or restart an automatic presentation.	S
End a presentation.	ESC
Erase on-screen annotations.	E
Go to the next slide, if the next slide is hidden.	H
Set new timings while rehearsing.	T
Re-record slide narration and timing	R
Return to the first slide.	Press and hold Left Mouse button for several seconds
Change the pointer to a pen.	Ctrl+P
Change the pointer to an arrow.	Ctrl+A
Change the pointer to an eraser	Ctrl+E
Show or hide ink markup	Ctrl+M
Hide the pointer and navigation button immediately.	Ctrl+H
Hide the pointer and navigation button in 15	Ctrl+U

seconds.	
View the **All Slides** dialog box	Ctrl+S
View the computer task bar	Ctrl+T
Display the shortcut menu.	Shift+F10
Go to the first or next hyperlink on the current slide.	Tab
Go to the last or previous hyperlink on the current slide.	Shift+Tab
Perform the "mouse click" behavior of the selected hyperlink. (Follow a selected hyperlink)	Enter while a hyperlink is selected

Control Video And Other Media During A Presentation.

These keyboard shortcuts work with video files imported from your computer or other device. They don't work with online video files.

During your presentation, if you want to see the list of media shortcuts, press F1. Then, in the **Slide Show Help** dialog box, go to the **Media** tab.

TASK	SHORTCUT
Stop media playback.	Alt+Q
Play or pause media.	Ctrl+Space
Toggle between play and pause.	Alt+P

Go to the next bookmark.	Alt+End
Go to the previous bookmark.	Alt+Home
Increase the sound volume.	Alt+Up
Decrease the sound volume.	Alt+Down
Seek forward.	Alt+Shift+Page Down
Seek backward.	Alt+Shift+Page Up
Mute the sound.	Alt+U

Keyboard Shortcuts For Smartart Graphics.

Insert a SmartArt graphic in an Office document

1. In the Microsoft Office program where you want to insert the graphic, press Alt, then N, and then M to open the **SmartArt Graphic** dialog box.
2. Press Up Arrow or Down Arrow to select the type of graphic that you want.
3. Press Tab to move to the Layout task pane.
4. Press the arrow keys to select the layout that you want.
5. Press Enter to insert the selected layout.

Work With Shapes In A SmartArt Graphic

TASK	SHORTCUT
Select the next element in a SmartArt graphic.	Tab
Select the previous element	Shift+Tab

in a SmartArt graphic.	
Select all shapes.	Ctrl +A
Remove focus from the selected shape.	Esc
Nudge the selected shape up.	Up Arrow
Nudge the selected shape down.	Down Arrow
Nudge the selected shape left.	Left Arrow
Nudge the selected shape right.	Right Arrow
Edit text in the selected shape.	Enter or F2, Esc to exit shape
Delete the selected shape.	Delete or Backspace
Cut the selected shape.	Ctrl+X or Shift+Delete
Copy the selected shape.	Ctrl+C
Paste the contents of the Clipboard.	Ctrl+V
Undo the last action.	Ctrl+Z

Move And Resize Shapes In A SmartArt Graphic

TASK	SHORTCUT
Enlarge the selected shape horizontally.	Shift+Right Arrow
Reduce the selected shape horizontally.	Shift+Left Arrow
Enlarge the selected shape vertically.	Shift+Up Arrow
Reduce the selected shape vertically.	Shift+Down Arrow

Rotate the selected shape to the right.	Alt+Right Arrow
Rotate the selected shape to the left.	Alt+Left Arrow

Notes:

- To apply more precise adjustments to shapes, press the Ctrl key in addition to any of the above keyboard shortcuts.
- These keyboard shortcuts apply to multiple selections as if you selected each item individually.

Work With Text In A SmartArt Graphic

TASK	SHORTCUT
Move one character to the left.	Left Arrow
Move one character to the right.	Right Arrow
Move up one line.	Up Arrow
Move down one line.	Down Arrow
Move one word to the left.	Ctrl+Left Arrow
Move one word to the right.	Ctrl+Right Arrow
Move one paragraph up.	Ctrl+Up Arrow
Move one paragraph down.	Ctrl+Down Arrow
Move to the end of a line.	End
Move to the beginning of a line.	Home
Move to the end of a text box.	Ctrl+End
Move to the beginning of a text box.	Ctrl+Home

Cut selected text.	Ctrl+X
Copy selected text.	Ctrl+C
Paste selected text.	Ctrl+V
Move the selected text up.	Alt+Shift+Up Arrow
Move the selected text down.	Alt+Shift+Down Arrow
Undo the last action.	Ctrl+Z
Delete one character to the left.	Backspace
Delete one word to the left.	Ctrl+Backspace
Delete one character to the right.	Delete
Delete one word to the right.	Ctrl+Delete
Promote the selected text.	Alt+Shift+Left Arrow
Demote the selected text.	Alt+Shift+Right Arrow
Check the spelling (not available in Word).	F7

Apply Character Formatting

TASK	SHORTCUT
Open the **Font** dialog box.	Ctrl+Shift+F or Ctrl+Shift+P
Increase the font size of the selected text.	Ctrl+Shift+>
Decrease the font size of the selected text.	Ctrl+Shift+<
Switch the case of selected text (lower case, Title Case, UPPER CASE).	Shift+F3
Apply bold formatting to the	Ctrl+B

selected text.	
Apply an underline to the selected text.	Ctrl+U
Apply italic formatting to the selected text.	Ctrl+I
Apply subscript formatting to the selected text.	Ctrl+Equal Sign
Apply superscript formatting to the selected text.	Ctrl+Shift+Plus Sign
Adjust the superscript/subscript offset up.	Ctrl+Alt+Shift+>
Adjust the superscript/subscript offset down.	Ctrl+Alt+Shift+<
Remove all character formatting from the selected text.	Shift+Ctrl+Spacebar

Copy Text Formatting

TASK	SHORTCUT
Copy formatting from the selected text.	Shift+Ctrl+C
Paste formatting to the selected text.	Shift+Ctrl+V

Apply Paragraph Formatting

TASK	SHORTCUT
Center a paragraph.	Ctrl+E
Justify a paragraph.	Ctrl+J
Left align a	Ctrl+L

paragraph.	
Right align a paragraph.	Ctrl+R
Demote a bullet point.	Tab or Alt+Shift+Right Arrow
Promote a bullet point.	Shift+Tab or Alt+Shift+Left Arrow

Use The Text Pane

TASK	SHORTCUT
Merge two lines of text.	Delete at the end of the first line of text
Display the shortcut menu.	Shift+F10
Switch between the **Text** pane and the drawing canvas.	Ctrl+Shift+F2
Close the **Text** pane.	Alt+F4
Switch the focus from the **Text** pane to the border of the SmartArt graphic.	Esc
Open the SmartArt graphics Help topic. (Your pointer should be in the Text pane.)	Ctrl +Shift+F1

☐

Use The Keyboard To Work With The Ribbon

Do tasks quickly without using the mouse by pressing a few keys—no matter where you are in an Office program. You can get to every command on the ribbon by using an access key—usually by pressing two to four keys.

1. Press and release the ALT key.

   You see the little boxes called KeyTips over each command available in the current view.

2. Press the letter shown in the KeyTip over the command you want to use.
3. Depending on which letter you pressed, you might see additional KeyTips. For example, if the **Home** tab is active and you pressed N, the **Insert** tab is displayed, along with the KeyTips for the groups in that tab.
4. Continue pressing letters until you press the letter of the specific command you want to use.

   Tip: To cancel the action you're taking and hide the KeyTips, press and release the ALT key.

Change the keyboard focus without using the mouse

Another way to use the keyboard to work with the ribbon is to move the focus among the tabs and commands until you find the feature you want to use. The following shows some ways to move the keyboard focus without using the mouse.

TASK	SHORTCUT
Select the active tab and show the access keys.	ALT or F10. Press either of these keys again to move back to the Office file and cancel the access keys.

Move to another tab.	ALT or F10 to select the active tab, and then LEFT ARROW or RIGHT ARROW.
Move to another Group on the active tab.	ALT or F10 to select the active tab, and then CTRL+RIGHT ARROW or LEFT ARROW to move between groups.
Minimize (collapse) or restore the ribbon.	CTRL+F1
Display the shortcut menu for the selected item.	SHIFT+F10
Move the focus to select the active tab, your Office file, task pane, or status bar.	F6
Move the focus to each command in the ribbon, forward or backward.	ALT or F10, and then TAB or SHIFT+TAB
Move down, up, left, or right among the items in the ribbon.	DOWN ARROW, UP ARROW, LEFT ARROW, or RIGHT ARROW
Go to the selected command or control in the ribbon.	SPACE BAR or ENTER
Open the selected menu or gallery in the ribbon.	SPACE BAR or ENTER
Go to a command or option in the ribbon so you can change it.	ENTER
Finish changing the value	ENTER

of a command or option in the ribbon, and move focus back to the Office file.	
Get help on the selected command or control in the ribbon. (If no Help article is associated with the selected command, the Help table of contents for that program is shown instead.)	F1

Customer's Page.

This page is for customers who enjoyed Microsoft PowerPoint 2016 Keyboard Shortcuts For Windows.

Dearly beloved customer, please leave a review behind if you enjoyed this book or found it helpful. It will be highly appreciated, thank you.

Other Books By This Publisher.

S/N	Title	Series
Series A: Limits Breaking Quotes.		
1	Discover Your Key Christian Quotes	Limits Breaking Quotes
Series B: Shortcut Matters.		
1	Windows 7 Shortcuts	Shortcut Matters
2	Windows 7 Shortcuts & Tips	Shortcut Matters
3	Windows 8.1 Shortcuts	Shortcut Matters
4	Windows 10 Shortcut Keys	Shortcut Matters
5	Microsoft Office 2007 Keyboard Shortcuts For Windows.	Shortcut Matters
6	Microsoft Office 2010 Shortcuts For Windows.	Shortcut Matters
7	Microsoft Office 2013 Shortcuts For Windows.	Shortcut Matters
Series C: Teach Yourself.		
1	Teach Yourself Computer Fundamentals	Teach Yourself
Series D: For Painless Publishing		
1	Self-Publish it with CreateSpace.	For Painless Publishing
2	Where is my money? Now solved for Kindle and CreateSpace	For Painless Publishing
3	Describe it on Amazon	For Painless Publishing
4	How To Market That Book.	For Painless Publishing